GW00786364

IRON K

By
JAMES STILL

Dramatic Publishing
Woodstock, Illinois • England • Australia • New Zealand

"I would argue that the future of our country hangs in the balance because the future of marriage hangs in the balance. Isn't that the ultimate homeland security, standing up and defending marriage?"

— Senator Rick Santorum
on the Gay Marriage Amendment as
reported by the Associated Press
on July 14, 2004.

* * *

A Mother's hardest to forgive.
Life is the fruit she longs to hand you,
Ripe on a plate. And while you live,
Relentlessly she understands you.

— Phyllis McGinley

IMPORTANT BILLING AND CREDIT REQUIREMENTS

NOTES FROM THE WRITER

I've often described writing plays as a kind of "accepting an invitation." Sometimes that invitation has come from the simplest image, sometimes from the emerging story, sometimes from the structure of the story, and always from a character who simply refuses my refusals.

Iron Kisses is a play about a brother and sister who play everyone in their family. Mostly they play their parents (as well as themselves) and while on the face of it this choice might risk seeming like a gimmick, I love the pure theatricality of it, the truth in the little details, and the shifting perspectives and point of view. But it's also emotionally true, that idea that no matter how much we might try, family is profoundly inescapable.

At its heart, *Iron Kisses* is about a family struggling to recognize itself as it's breathlessly changing and evolving in ways unimaginable not just fifty years ago, but even ten years ago. It's about that nagging sense that we all, at one critical time or another, "become" our parents. But it's also about grief, about the ways we grieve, about our need to be with people we love when we're grieving, even if we don't know how to do it. Grief is lonely. It's also messy. By the time we get to the end of *Iron Kisses* and realize how the end of the play is also the beginning of the play—the characters' grief makes meaning out of everything that's come before.

While it's up to a director and the actors to make any production personal and fully realized on their own terms, not surprisingly I have some big fat opinions about how the play works best. In no particular order:

— The transitions that Billy and Barbara make as they go back and forth between playing both Mom and Dad should be simple and clear. Audiences get it. It's about essence...less really is more.

— I prefer that the play be produced without an intermission. It's designed to play straight through (at about 90 minutes) which not only serves the story but is also my love letter to actors who can remarkably transform themselves (and us) as story-tellers and characters.

— Music can be very helpful throughout. It's delicate—but definitely worth the trouble.

Finally: I started writing *Iron Kisses* while a writer in residence at The New Harmony Project in southern Indiana. One morning during my residency, I was at breakfast and shared a table with a handful of folks—including the four-year old son of one of the dramaturgs there that summer. The dramaturg (Diane) told me a story of how her son Corey had recently drawn a self-portrait which included hair of happiness. When I heard Corey's story, I felt something crack open inside my heart, I couldn't get back to my play soon enough, and within days I had finished the first scene of the play. With Corey's permission, I've included a copy of his self-portrait. Thank you, Corey. You and your story are proof that plays can reveal themselves in the most mysterious—and surprising ways.

— James Still

Drawing by Corey Brewer Rigney

Deepest thanks to People's Light & Theatre Company for workshop and development support of *Iron Kisses*: David Bradley, Michael Cruz, Jeep, Shannon O'Donnell, Kathryn Petersen.

Thanks to The New Harmony Project for giving me a quiet place to start writing this play at the 2004 conference where I was a writer in residence.

More deep thanks to Marge Betley and Geva Theatre Center for providing workshop and development support as part of Hibernatus Interruptus. Special thanks to Peter Amster, Ryan Artzberger, Jen Kern and Frank Cavallo.

IRON KISSES premiered at Geva Theatre Center, Mark Cuddy, artistic director, in Rochester, New York, on March 17, 2006. Direction was by Stephanie Gilman, scenic design by Wilson Chin, costume design by Anne R. Emo, lighting design by S. Ryan Schmidt, sound design by Daniel Baker, original music by Matthew Suttor and the Broken Chord Collective and dramaturgy by Marge Betley. The stage manager was Alexandra M. Backus. The cast was:

BARBARA . . . . Mary Bacon
BILLY . . . . Jacob Blumer

* * * *

IRON KISSES was a winner of The Arch and Bruce Brown Foundation Prize for Playwriting.

IRON KISSES

A Play in One Act

CHARACTERS:

BILLY . . . . mid-30s to 40s
BARBARA . . . . mid-30s to 40s

SETTING: A small town in the Midwest and San Francisco.
TIME: Now.

Scene 1: Iron Kisses
Scene 2: The Long Division of My Mother
Scene 3: Happiness Is What You Can Bear

For Bonnie

IRON KISSES

SCENE ONE:

In the dark we hear the old Fifth Dimension recording of Laura Nyro's "The Wedding Bell Blues," or something similar. As the song builds, we begin to see slides from weddings, lots of different weddings from different eras—like a family scrapbook. Brides and grooms that sheepishly look toward the camera with hope and fear. Wedding dresses that mark the changing styles of a century. The pictures might include a bride and groom feeding each other wedding cake, the iconic image of the bride and groom kissing on the "You may kiss the bride" cue, the bride and groom flanked by both sets of parents, a line of bridesmaids, etc. Suddenly there is a photo of two men. They are arm in arm, smiling giddily, both in tuxes. It's the 21st century. At first glance they might be mistaken for two groomsmen, two friends, two brothers even. But the photo dissolves very slowly into another photo: the same two men are kissing on the mouth. It's romantic and tender. The Fifth Dimension are fading away—and the image blurs—but it never disappears completely. The photo of the two men kissing might remain in ghostly view throughout the rest of the scene.

Lights bloom onstage to reveal A MAN—he's one of the kissing men in the photo. Onstage, he might be sitting in

11

a chair. He's holding a medium-sized beautiful wooden box. You know if he opens the box that the air will fill with the scents of long ago, with fingerprints, with hope.

He slowly opens the box and looks inside, pulling out a stamped, handwritten, opened envelope.

BILL'S MOM. Well...it's a wedding invitation. Anyone can see that. It came in the mail mixed up with a VISA bill, and a newsletter from my church, a couple of offers for unlimited night minutes if you switch to a different long-distance carrier, and a two-dollar coupon off a certain brand of cheese. I saw the wedding invitation right away because it was the only envelope with a hand-written address. Have you noticed how we just don't get that much handwritten mail anymore? Everyone's just so busy. *(She turns the wedding invitation over and over in her hands. Then, discovery:)* The stamp is one of those "LOVE" stamps. My son used to collect stamps. He'd say that getting a stamp from some far-away country made him feel like he'd get to go there someday. *(Beat. Looking at the wedding invitation.)* It was the handwriting that I recognized. It's my son's handwriting. *(From the wooden box, she pulls out a child's drawing, worn and fragile.)* He probably doesn't want me to tell you this, but for years I kept a picture that Billy drew for me when he was a little boy... For years it hung on our refrigerator, next to football and basketball schedules. It's Billy's self-portrait. All around the face there's these squiggly yellow lines, see, which I thought was supposed to be his hair. But Billy had dark hair so I asked him why he had drawn his self-portrait with yellow hair.

And Billy said, "That isn't my hair, Mom. That's my happiness." He signed it, "To Mommy—Love, Billy." *(She gives the drawing to someone sitting in the audience.)* You can just pass it around. I would like it back when you've looked at it though.

(When she returns to her chair, she turns around and is someone else. Maybe he assumes a different posture, maybe a slightly different voice—but not with a lot of effort. It's the story that's important.)

BILL'S DAD *(holding the wedding invitation)*. When I got home from work that day, there was the usual stack of mail waiting for me on the kitchen table, just like any other day. My wife always puts the mail in order of how she thinks I'll want to read it. And on the bottom of the pile there was this unopened envelope. It was from my son. *(He looks at the invitation.)* Billy—Bill—he always had very distinctive handwriting. Not feminine—just distinctive. When he was first learning how to write in cursive, must have been in the third or fourth grade, he used to spend hours on his handwriting. He'd fill up pages and pages with his cursive handwriting. If you asked him what he was doing, he'd just say, "Practicing." One night after the kids had gone to bed and I was still up watching Johnny Carson on the TV, my wife came in with the funniest look on her face. She'd been picking up after the kids, in one hand she was holding Barbara's baton, in the other hand was a notebook that Billy had been writing in that day… I remember the guests on Johnny Carson that night were Captain Kangaroo and Rock Hudson.

(He shifts in his seat again, becoming BILL's MOM again.)

BILL'S MOM. I was never the kind of mom who went around snooping in their kids' private stuff, you know. But this was just a notebook, Billy was just a little boy, he liked to practice his handwriting. I don't even think I meant to look at it—maybe Billy wanted me to see it, or maybe God did—because it just fell open and I saw pages and pages of this notebook filled with Billy's perfect eight-year-old handwriting. It was the same phrase written over and over and over again. It said— *(Pausing, then slow, like she's reading a foreign language:)* "BILLY LOVES JASON." Pages and pages of that. *(Beat.)* "BILLY LOVES JASON." *(Beat.)* Well that was a long time ago. Unbelievably long time ago. *(Beat. Then very direct:)* I don't have a problem with Billy being gay—I really don't. It's the fact that he loves men that makes me uncomfortable.

(He shifts again, becoming BILL's DAD.)

BILL'S DAD. When Billy told me about, you know, when he told me that he was—you know, homosexual, I asked him when it happened, you know, I asked him when he turned that way, when he knew. He told me he'd ALWAYS been "that way"—he'd always been gay. Billy told me that he can't remember NOT being gay, that he's been gay forever. "Even when you were a little kid?" "Dad, when you're a little kid, you don't ask yourself if you're gay, you just know who you love." The thing about that that I just find impossible to understand is that I don't know how I didn't know. I mean, all those years watching him and thinking one thing—and then finding out later that it was something completely different all along. That HE—my son was—something completely different. I just never imagined it, not one of my own kids, I guess. It just doesn't seem possible that your child can keep a secret for such a long time. And then of course you wonder what else you might have missed, what other secrets the world is keeping from you.

BILL'S MOM. I used to have this dream, I had the same dream several times. It was a wedding. And Billy was the groom. And the bride was some girl—I didn't know her in the dream, she was just this nice girl with blonde hair. You knew they were going to have beautiful children. People always say that weddings are really for the parents. That's one of the things about all this gay marriage stuff—I don't think those gay weddings are for the PARENTS. I think it's for the people who are getting married! And that just scares me. My problem is that I really do like Billy—I do! I like who he is and how he turned out. Most parents only dream about having a son like Billy. You can imagine them saying stuff like, "My son is perfect, I wouldn't change a thing about him." Well when we say that we don't really mean that our kids are perfect. We just mean that we're proud of how they turned out. And I AM proud of Billy, I am. And I wish I could say I wouldn't change a thing about him. But secretly, I wish he was exactly the way he is— just not gay. I told Billy that one time when we were going through a difficult period with him, I told him I wish you could be exactly who you are—but not gay! I said I wasn't trying to hurt him, I was just being honest. He told me that if I loved him, then I loved him because he IS gay, and that I couldn't have it both ways—because it's just WHO HE IS...and then he said he wasn't trying to hurt me he was just being honest. We didn't talk again after that for about six months.

BILL'S DAD. Billy and Michael have lived together for years. They—they met at the gym. They were both lifting weights. Billy says that on Monday they did backs and biceps; Wednesday was legs day; Friday was shoulders and triceps; and on Sunday they moved in together. They've been inseparable ever since. We've had them in our home, they visit us when they can. They're both very busy. Billy had brought a couple of his other friends home to meet us over the years. But I never cared for them much. It was difficult to find anything to talk about and I hate to admit it but it was always a relief when they'd leave. It was different with Michael. Michael made it impossible for us not to like him. We liked him from the moment we saw him. That surprised me. What surprised me more was that when I saw them together that first time—they looked like a couple. I don't know how to explain that, I don't think I've ever really known a couple—men, in a couple, I mean; a gay couple. I've never known one, or known that I knew one. But Billy and Michael—they just...that surprised me.

(BILL's MOM jumps right in:)

BILL'S MOM. I was a little less impressed with Michael than my husband was. On the outside, I'm the one who's more outgoing. But on the inside, I'm pretty careful. Especially when it comes to my children. I don't like watching them do things they're going to regret later. It's awful not being able to save 'em, not being able to help them save themselves. And I didn't trust Michael. I was worried that Billy was going to get hurt. You could see that Billy thought the world of him, the way he laughed at things Michael would say, or, the way he'd look in my direction full of hope-hope-hoping that I'd like Michael. That first night, the four of us were sitting around the table having dinner. I got up to see about dessert, and when I looked back, I could see that under the table—Billy and Michael were holding hands. I realized that even though I'd known about Billy—you know, that he's gay—I'd known that for years by then—but I had never thought about Billy touching another man—like, that, I mean, like—holding hands. I'd thought about other things—you know, sexual things—I'd thought about that, not the details, not what they DID, but I'd wondered about it, you know, about sex and Billy. I mean, not all the time, I didn't obsess about it, but when Billy told me he was gay I thought about—well I watch the news. You just—worry. And I guess I was so busy worrying that I never thought about Billy holding hands with another man. *(She stops. Beat.)* I didn't say very much the rest of that evening. I know Billy was disappointed that I was so quiet. I know he thought that I didn't like Michael. But I was trying to remember the last time that my husband held MY hand…

(BILL's MOM drifts off in thought. BILL's DAD picks up the story.)

BILL'S DAD. Something I never told Billy, although it was pretty obvious, is that I was nervous when we met them together that first time. With Billy's sister Barbara, I always pretended I didn't really like the guy because if I seemed to like him TOO much then she'd lose interest in him for sure. But if I acted like I didn't think much of the guy at all then she'd be telling us that she wanted to marry him. I got real good at just staying, you know, right in the middle. Right there, in the middle. But Billy is a different kind of kid—he never seemed to be so serious about someone before, the way he was with Michael. So I just didn't have much practice. It was like Billy was a teenager dating for the first time and we were the parents—which we should have known how to do, but it was different somehow. It was like we'd skipped over that part of Billy's life and I just didn't know what the rules were, I didn't know how I was supposed to act. I also didn't want to embarrass Billy in front of his friend and I didn't want them to embarrass me and Billy's mother either. It was very confusing. We were all grownups but it felt like none of us knew what we were doing. Michael said "please" and "thank you"—I remember that. He had a strong handshake, I remember that too. He didn't wear an earring which I was sorta happy about. He took a second piece of cake even though my wife had made better before. At one point I wondered about Michael's parents, who they were, what they did, whether or not they loved their son. And what they thought about MY son.

(BILL's DAD gives up trying to explain it. BILL's MOM resumes her side of things:)

BILL'S MOM. We live in a town where there's just not many people in our exact situation. I mean, folks don't celebrate "Gay Pride" here in the summer, it's not one of the big holidays. But they're proud of other things, they're proud of their kids. They go to baseball games and take the kids to the swimming pool. People work in their gardens and share tomatoes and zucchinis with each other. Farmers in their pickups wave with one finger. There are a lot of garage sales in the summer, kids sell lemonade at the side of the road. It's just all pretty normal. That's how Billy grew up too—he did all those things, he was in the middle of it, he belonged here. Sometimes it feels like Billy didn't just move away, sometimes it feels like he's dead. Not to me. But to the people in my town. They just gradually stopped asking about him. Every little thing I told them seemed to raise an eyebrow. I used to tell my husband that if folks here raised their eyebrows any higher they'd come right off their face. *(She is suddenly sitting in church.)* Sometimes in church I'll look around at the other people who still come. It's a lot of older folks. Most of the younger ones have moved away, and the ones that stay don't seem very interested in church. My daughter Barbara never comes to church. Even our ministers don't stay long, we get a new one every couple of years. I wonder if any of the people in my church are gay. I wonder if some of their kids are gay. I wonder what they'd do if somebody wanted to get married right here in our church, somebody who was gay. I'm a Methodist. But the story in my family goes that my grandparents were Catholic. That's Billy's great-grandparents. And when the Catholic church burned down they just walked across the street to the only other church in their little town, and that's how we became Methodists. If God was testing them—I'm not sure if that meant they passed the test or not. I suppose it depends on whether God turns out to be a Catholic or a Methodist. But they proved they could CHANGE. They passed THAT test anyway.

(BILL's DAD continues:)

BILL'S DAD. Another time when Billy and Michael were visiting, Billy had gotten up real early, earlier than me even. He'd made coffee and was reading our local newspaper. He still reads the sports page first. When he was growing up, Billy was the paperboy in our town, so he was always the first one awake. Not just in our family—but in the whole town. During the week he'd deliver the papers on his bike, waking up the town with the news of the day. On Sundays, the papers were so big, and he had so many extra customers that there was no way he could carry them all on his bike. So every Sunday I'd get up early with him and help him roll those papers, drive him around town, delivering the news. Some of those Sundays we hardly said a word, not because we were sore at each other, but because it was such a quiet time of the day. In the winter it'd still be dark; in the summer it wouldn't be hot yet. Sometimes we'd talk. One time Billy asked me if "eternity" and "forever" meant the same thing. I really didn't know what to say. And then Billy said: "Maybe ETERNITY is more like a place—and FOREVER more of a feeling." The morning when he said that, I knew that he'd grow up and move away. I knew that he wasn't going to find eternity or forever in our little town. I started to miss him that day—and he hadn't even left.

(BILL's DAD looks out at the audience like he's searching the vista. BILL's MOM takes over:)

BILL'S MOM. Billy's the first one to tell you that relationships aren't easy. One of the biggest burdens for him and Michael is that their friends all think they're perfect—the perfect couple—that they never fight, that they never have to work at it. One time the phone rang at home in the middle of the night—I shot up out of bed, my heart was already in my throat. Nobody calls with good news in the middle of the night, that's just one of those rules a mother lives by. It was Billy on the phone. He was crying. He and Michael had had a terrible fight. Michael decided to go out for a walk, get some air. Billy went after him. He got to the street just in time to see Michael step in front of a car that was going the wrong way down their one-way street. Billy was calling from the hospital. He was crying: *(BILLY:)* "No, Mom, you're not listening! They won't let me in to see him, they won't let me BE with Michael." That's why Billy was crying. Someone who didn't know those two boys told Billy he wasn't family and that they couldn't let him in to be with Michael. He was scared that Michael was going to die and never know that Billy was standing right outside his door. Billy would talk and then start crying again. He remembered that the car that had hit Michael was a '69 Impala. I didn't know what to say. I told him what my mother always told me: "things will be better in the morning, things are always better in the morning..." But he was completely undone, just a mess. I felt very far away. It's a side of Billy that I hadn't seen or heard since he was a boy, that messy, out of control side. When I told him that later he laughed and said that by the time he was twelve, he decided that the best way to make up for being gay, was to be perfect in every other way. If people liked everything else about him, then maybe they'd forgive him for being gay. Then he asked me if I'VE forgiven him. "Have you forgiven me for being gay? Mom?" I told him the truth. I forgave him a long time ago. It's ME that I still haven't forgiven.

BILL'S DAD. Of course we blamed ourselves. For years. I think that's pretty normal, most parents blame themselves, figure it's something they did. Billy said that he could almost live with that—that idea that he's gay because of something that we did. But his problem is that what we're really saying is that Billy is gay because of something that we did WRONG. *(He sighs.)* At night I lay in the dark and think about—you know I used wonder about how Billy could be our son, I mean how could he have come from us? Maybe we got the wrong kid. And it occurred to me one night that maybe we DIDN'T get the wrong kid, maybe he just got the wrong parents. I mean, take this marriage thing... If you ask me—and I know nobody did—but there's something about it that just doesn't feel right to me. Call me old-fashioned, I just can't quite understand it. I want my son to be happy, I do. I want him to have somebody in his life. I want him to feel loved. I want the world for him. But a wedding? What are we going tell our friends? Are we supposed to put a picture of Billy and Michael in the local paper with the other couples who get married? Should we ask our friends to send them a toaster or an electric can-opener?

BILL'S MOM. When Billy and Michael first started talking about getting married—I was careful not to say anything negative but I was thinking, "Well at least they can't REALLY get married, at least we're not going to have to deal with that too." And then all of a sudden there was all that stuff in the news, you couldn't turn around without someone on the TV talking about Massachusetts or San Francisco, things just started happening too fast. It was like we went to bed one night and woke up the next morning in a totally different world. WE were exactly the same but the world was totally different. Then Billy called and said that he and Michael were thinking pretty seriously about getting married—to each other! I tried to change the subject, tried to tell him a story about Barbara's kids—but Billy interrupted me and asked if we'd come to their wedding if they paid for our plane tickets and...I—I just couldn't get time to slow down enough for me to get my arms around it. I asked Billy:

"Why do you have to get married? Why can't you just have one of those—those civil union things?"

"Mom. I guess we don't want to be civil. We want to be outrageous, we want to be passionate. We want to be married."

"Billy—"

"I'm not asking for your permission, Mom. I'm asking you to come to my wedding."

I couldn't breathe.

"Mom?"

"I'm here."

"Well don't decide now. Think about it. Talk it over with Dad. It won't be the same if you and Dad don't come. I'd really like you to be there."

"Well what about Michael's parents—won't they be there?"

"No."

There was this long pause. And then Billy said it again:

"No. They said no."

I was surprised about Michael's parents, we'd never met them but Billy had always told us they were so great. They lived on the East Coast. I always had this fantasy about them in my head, that they were everything that Billy's father and I couldn't be. Or wouldn't be. I suppose it was in that moment that I knew we had the chance to be mother and father to both of them. I hadn't felt needed by Billy for so long that I forgot that he might need us for ANYTHING. *(Angry:)* I just wish it wasn't for THIS. *(Beat.)* In some ways Billy never asked for very much from us—but in other ways he asked for everything. *(She looks at the wedding invitation again.)*

BILL'S DAD. When I was looking in the Yellow Pages for a travel agent, I noticed there are more divorce lawyers than there are wedding planners. We went back and forth about whether or not we'd go. Neither me or my wife had ever been to San Francisco. I just couldn't imagine how big the Pacific Ocean must look. My wife admitted that she kind of wanted to see the Golden Gate

Bridge. Neither one of us had traveled that much, and we surely hadn't been on an airplane for several years, not since September 11th. One of the pretty flight attendants asked us what we were going to do in San Francisco. I told her we were going to our son's wedding. My wife choked on her ginger-ale when I said that. We hadn't told anyone back home why we were going. Folks thought it was strange enough that we were going to California.

BILL'S MOM. I have this picture in my head from the wedding. It was after the ceremony was over, there was music coming from someplace. My husband had gone to get us something warm to drink. It was starting to rain. Someone offered me an umbrella. I stood there alone, the sound of the rain drowning out the music. I looked around for Billy. He and Michael had wandered away from the crowd. They were standing with their arms around each other. They were kissing. It was raining hard now, but for some reason it didn't seem to be raining on Billy and Michael. There was this golden light all around them. Yellow squiggly lines. It wasn't the sun. It was their happiness.

(As the lights begin to fade, the faint photo of the two men kissing comes back into focus, gets stronger and stronger. The lights go out, the photo remains. And then it disappears, like someone exhaling.)

END OF SCENE ONE

SCENE TWO:
The Long Division of My Mother (a mathematical problem)

In the dark we hear Tony Bennett singing the classic "I Left My Heart in San Francisco," or something similar. Then we begin to see images/snapshots of San Francisco...pictures taken by a tourist, there might be a finger partially blocking one or two of the photos. There's nothing particularly beautiful about the photos, more importantly they are proof that someone was there, someone saw these things through the lens of a camera.

The last photo fades away into a shot of clouds and fog.

FLIGHT ATTENDANT *(V.O.)*. "Please return your seats to their original upright positions and make sure that all carry-on items are stowed in the overhead compartments or under the seat in front of you."

(Lights come up onstage to reveal a WOMAN sitting on a big suitcase. She's going through a shopping bag full of trinkets, T-shirts, tourist stuff, some of it wrapped in tissue paper. She's checking the items against receipts, carefully making notes in pen, adding up dollar amounts.)

BARBARA'S MOM. Well a mother can't divide herself up as easily as she divides the Christmas presents. I've always been fair, always saved all the receipts at Christmas and made sure that I spent EXACTLY the same amount on both of my kids. Now I do it for my grandkids...birthdays, special occasions. Everyone's equal, everyone gets the same amount. To the penny. And I keep the receipts to prove it. *(Determined:)* I love them all exactly the same. I do. Even when it doesn't feel that way—I do. I do! One Christmas—this was a long time ago, both of my kids were still living at home, they must have been in high school—we had opened all the presents, I even made eggnog that year. My son Billy was already listening to his new Elton John album, trying on one of his new sweaters. But my daughter Barbara looked put out, like something was missing. I assured her that Santa had spent exactly the same on her and her brother. "No, Mom, it's nothing like that." "Well what is then? Don't you like your presents?" And Barbara looked at me with the most serious look on her face and said, "Mom! What I really wanted for Christmas was larger breasts." I knew better than to flinch, I didn't even move, we just stared at each other. Finally Barbara laughed that way she always laughs when she's pleased with herself—the way she STILL laughs when she's pleased with herself. I just wiped eggnog from her face and said, "Maybe next year, honey."

BARBARA'S DAD. Barbara and her mother have always had a hard time. I don't know what you call it—complicated, I guess. Don't get me wrong—they're close; ask anyone and they'd tell you that Barbara and her mother are close. Between you and me, they're an awful lot alike—which is something that Barbara can't really understand because she just thinks of her mother as her mother... I mean, if you ask me—and I know nobody did—but a big part of their problem is that they're just too much alike. But don't say that to my wife or she'll surely blow a gasket. And to make things worse, it's never been that complicated between me and Barbara. Or we were able to keep it UNcomplicated. Something about fathers and daughters, I guess... There's no competition. Barbara and her mother—it's always about who's right, who wins. The thing is, I've learned a lot from living with my wife for all these years, I can just tell when she's in one of her moods, I know when to stay out of her way. It's the same with my daughter. I just stay out of the way. You learn these things, it doesn't take a rocket scientist to figure it out. Things get crazy I just find something to do, I become invisible.

BARBARA'S MOM. It still irritates me how my husband just disappears whenever Barbara gets in one of her moods. She'll be on her high horse about something— Republicans or the school system, or the dangers of too many X-rays—and I'm left to take her on all by myself. I'm looking around for my husband, for support, but he's slipped away, disappeared right when I need him. And just try having a normal conversation with Barbara. We're complete opposites. She loves to argue, she loves to argue with ME, loves to argue with me about EVERYTHING—and I hate to argue. And she knows I hate to argue and when I won't argue back she tells me how angry I am about everything and THEN I get angry. I get angry about her always telling me how angry I am about everything! *(Calming down:)* I worry that I'm harder on Barbara than I am on Billy. But Billy moved away—or "got away" as Barbara likes to remind me. She married John, they went to high school together, I don't think it ever occurred to John to leave the area. Well I suppose it's natural for a mother to be more in awe of her son than her daughter. Mothers and daughters are just more equal, there's less mystery. Everyone says that Barbara and I look alike and I suppose there's some truth to that. But people don't get along just because they look alike. My word, I feel like I've been arm wrestling Barbara since she was a baby. *(She takes a T-shirt out of the bag and shows it off to the audience.)* We have two grandkids—Barbara's kids. A girl and a little boy. I got this cute T-shirt for the boy: *(Reading the T-shirt, tickled with herself:)* "My Grandma Went to San Francisco and All I Got Was This Lousy T-Shirt." I think he'll like it. It's bound to shrink when we wash it so I got a medium.

BARBARA'S DAD. When my wife and I made the trip to San Francisco, my watch stopped working. It was the funniest thing to be without a watch. Plus it's another time zone out there in California. At first I was always looking at my watch and adding the number of hours to their time so I'd know the real time, the time it was back at home. And then my watch broke so I couldn't keep track of the time there or here. My father gave me this watch when I got married. He said that a good watch makes a good man. It's run like a dream all these years. Only had problems with it two times. Once was out there in San Francisco—it broke on me, at Billy and Michael's thing. The first time was when my daughter Barbara got married. My watch stopped working right before I was to walk her down the aisle. I kept tapping on it trying to get it going again, until Barbara said to me, "Dad, it's time! It's time to walk me down the aisle." Maybe I was trying to stop time, you know. Maybe I was just hoping to keep my kids young. Getting older is a funny thing, it's not at all like I thought it would be. You don't need a watch to tell you you're getting old, that's for sure. I see my kids getting older—I figure I must be getting older too.

BARBARA'S MOM. Things between us and Barbara's husband were difficult from the beginning. Barbara seemed to get a kick out of that part of it. I hope she didn't marry him just to spite us—I feel bad even saying that, but it did cross my mind. I don't like watching my kids doing things they're going to regret later. It's awful not being able to save 'em, awful not being able to help them save themselves. But Barbara was determined to marry him and I guess I was determined to let her. I remember the reception line after Barbara's wedding and Billy came through shaking all our hands, acting like a goofball, just playing around. But when he got to Barbara he grabbed her and they held onto each other real tight. They were both crying—holding onto each other—brother and sister. I felt kind of jealous of that, of how close they were. I think they both knew that there was no turning back. In a way it was the end of their childhood, Barbara's wedding. And in another way it was the first time I felt old.

BARBARA'S DAD. Barbara and the kids picked us up at the airport when we flew back from California. I was happy to get home, let me tell you...I just wanted to sleep in my own bed, read my own little newspaper. In San Francisco I kept checking to see if part of the paper was missing, the part that had anything to do with me. You'd think that news is news but the news out there didn't seem to have much to do with my life. *(Beat. He sits in the chair. He's suddenly riding in a car, looking out the window.)* It sure is a long drive from the airport to our place.

BARBARA'S MOM. The drive home is typical with Barbara and her kids. They make more noise than a marching band, and there's fights about whose turn it is to sit up front with their mom, and what radio station we'll listen to, and the little one is repeating everything the older one is saying word-for-word just to be annoying, word-for-word just to be annoying. Barbara doesn't seem to get as irritated with her son the same way she does with her daughter—and I wonder if she favors him. Did I favor Billy when they were growing up? No, I don't think I did. I think I tried to love them equally—even when they weren't equally lovable.

BARBARA'S DAD. There's snow on the ground, the interstate is just fields on both sides. It looks awful flat compared to how it was in San Francisco. The sky looks bigger here. I can feel us driving toward something familiar, it's like being pulled real hard by a magnet—I don't know how else to describe it—it's like I expect to see myself waiting for me when I get home. *(Suddenly self-conscious:)* Boy I'm tired! And that sounds like another time zone talking.

BARBARA'S MOM. The grandkids are still fighting about wanting to sit up front so I settle the argument once and for all by declaring that I will be sitting up front all the way home. This doesn't stop Barbara and her daughter from starting up again in some fight they've been having for years even though none of us can remember what it's about—and I just sit back and watch them. Who does Barbara remind me of? MY mother? No. Barbara sounds just like me, and her daughter sounds just like

Barbara. So who do I sound like? *(Beat.)* Barbara looks pretty, tired but pretty. She's prettier than I ever was. But she seems sad. I don't remember feeling sad when I was Barbara's age. Thinking I'm being nice, I comment on my granddaughter's short hair—and Barbara quickly lets me know that I've said the wrong thing…that she had cut her hair herself, had just taken a pair of scissors and chopped off her ponytail. For no good reason! My granddaughter smooths down her hair and repeats how much she LIKES it short and how everyone at school thinks her hair looks COOL and my grandson is once again repeating everything his sister says, "everyone at school thinks her hair looks COOL…" My husband is snoring in the backseat. He's fallen asleep looking out the window…

BARBARA'S DAD. My wife thinks I'm sleeping, but I hear everything that's being said. Barbara is always saying she's going to get a divorce so when she says it in the car I don't really think much about it.

BARBARA'S MOM. I have never heard Barbara use the word "divorce" before. I mean, I know Barbara and John have had their share of problems, but…

BARBARA'S DAD. I've never understood why folks get divorced. I mean, you get divorced—and then what? What happens to you? Who do you spend your time with? Who do you talk to? Most of the couples our age, the ones we know—they're divorced. They tell us that they just couldn't stay married any longer. But after they divorce they still don't seem any happier to me. One fella I know, about my age, when his wife left him he just stopped, just like my watch stopped. He just stopped doing anything, just became a tired old man overnight.

Stopped coming to church, stopped coming to the high school basketball games, stopped coming in to town altogether. His hair turned white—like he'd seen a ghost.

BARBARA'S MOM. Well when Barbara says divorce that first time it makes me feel sick inside. Part of me is sad of course, part of me worries about the kids. And part of me is relieved because there's still time for Barbara to have a good life. And part of me is just mad about the whole thing! Maybe I am a little bit angry. I feel all those things. I guess that's something that having kids does to you—all the stretch marks make room for more feelings. But Barbara is talking about divorce like it isn't anything special, you know, like if I turn down the sound and just watch her mouth move I'm gonna think she's talking about something she saw on TV, or about the three-day weather forecast, something plain like that. I'm trying so hard to listen to what she says that I miss most of what she says. Then it gets quiet for a long time. Even the kids are quiet. And Barbara is crying real soft, staring straight ahead as she drives. I ask her if she's OK, and she shakes her head and turns on the radio. Some love song starts playing on the oldies station—it's just so predictable. Songs like that always play at the exact wrong moment, songs about loving someone forever and never feeling this way before, and how did I ever live without you and stuff. Barbara must have heard it too because she starts laughing, shaking her head, laughing, only tears are still coming down her face. I don't feel much like laughing but I force myself so she'll know that I'm trying. I surprise her by singing along with the lyrics of that song. She's impressed that I know the song—and I don't have the heart to tell her that I don't really know the song, it's just that the words are so predictable... Barbara starts to sing along too. Our voices don't really blend very good, but I guess that isn't the point. In an odd way, things were so much simpler in San Francisco than right now, here, at home.

BARBARA'S DAD. I'm fiddling with my watch when we finally get off the interstate and turn onto the two-lane road that will take us home. It's not much further now. Barbara and her mother finally stop singing. Me and the grandkids are in the back, the little one has wiggled out of his seatbelt and is trying to sit on my lap, pulling on my ears so I'll stick out my tongue— *(He demonstrates.)* It's a game we've played since he was a little baby. It used to make him laugh, now he just does it to pass the time. My granddaughter is reading an old book she found in our basement called *Valley of the Dolls*. She never liked playing with dolls when she was little. When they start singing up in the front again she says they are so gay and puts her earphones back on her head. The car suddenly swerves, Barbara and my wife are screaming, my grandson holds tight to my neck, and I get a bad feeling in my stomach. There's this loud thick flat sound of something hitting the car—hard. This all happens— *(snapping his fingers)* —like that. Barbara brings the car to a stop on the side of the road. I get out and follow a short trail of blood to where a big deer is laying off to the side of the road. We'd hit it square on, it's dead. Nothing for us to do but leave it there and get home. The coyotes will take care of it. There's a big dent in the hood. One of the headlights is broke. But nobody's hurt, just shook up. The clouds cover the moon and everyone's quiet as we start back down the road again.

BARBARA'S MOM. My grandson leans up and asks his mom how do you drive at night when it's so dark... Barbara tells him that's why you have headlights, they help you see in the dark. He's quiet and then leans back up and says, "But Mom, we only have one headlight, how do you know we're still on the road???" Barbara says in the softest voice I ever heard her use, "There's just enough light to get us home, sweetie; just enough, that's all we need."

BARBARA'S DAD. And we did get home. I got outa the car and kissed the sidewalk that leads up to our front door. The kids thought I was being funny.

BARBARA'S MOM. First thing I did was call Billy to let him know we got home OK. I was doing what I had always wanted HIM to do—just letting him know that we got home OK. I can't tell you how much sleep I've lost over the years worrying about my kids, hoping they were home safe, in bed, safe. *(Realization:)* All these years when I thought of my kids like that—I always pictured Billy in bed, alone. Now I'd have to try and put Michael in that picture too. With Barbara I always just assumed she was in bed with John. And now it seemed like I might have to work on cutting him out of that picture.

BARBARA'S DAD. Barbara wants a turn to talk on the phone, she wants to say hi to Michael. She talked so easily to Michael, like she'd known him her whole life. She laughed at something he said, and I could hear Michael laughing too. My daughter is talking to my son's—husband. *(Beat.)* So this is my family… My parents would never have believed this.

BARBARA'S MOM. I was on the extension— *(Guilty:)* I didn't hang up the phone, I knew I should, I knew it was wrong…but I listened to Barbara and Billy talking, holding my breath, afraid I'd get caught but unable to hang up the phone. I wanted to know what they talked about—when they thought I wasn't listening.

(THE TELEPHONE CALL: BILLY appears in another part of the stage. He can't see what we can: that BARBARA is having a difficult time keeping it together.)

PHONE CALL

BARBARA *(laughter, then)*. "Uh-huh and how'd Mom and Dad do?"

BILLY. "They were great. They seemed scared, but they were there, you know. I wish you coulda been there too."

BARBARA. "I know, I wanted to— *(Almost breaking down, trying to recover.)* Just—couldn't now." *(Beat.)*

BILLY. "Barb? *(Beat.)* You still there?"

BARBARA. "Can I call you back in a little bit? I need to get home, need to get the kids to bed. I want to talk to you."

BILLY. "Yeah, sure. You sure you're OK?"

BARBARA. "Did Mom look old to you?"

BILLY. "Old? I don't think so. No. Mom looks beautiful. Mom looks like Jackie Kennedy and Elizabeth Taylor, just like she always did."

BARBARA'S MOM. I don't know if that's what he really said. That's what I WANTED him to say. But I hung up the phone before I could hear the rest:

BARBARA. "Did Mom look old to you?"

BILLY. "Old? I don't—"

(The phone is hung up. BILLY exits.)

BARBARA'S DAD. Barbara and the kids finally went home, they live in our town, we'll see them tomorrow. Finally the house is ours again, finally quiet, finally just us, just the two of us. *(Lights begin to click off, one at a time.)* I go through the house and turn off all the lights, my shadow getting smaller and smaller as the house gets darker and darker. The last light I turn off is the porch light. *(The faint image of clouds gives way to a vast black winter sky, hard stars, a moon.)* Through the big picture window, I see lots of stars. *(Realization:)* We hadn't seen any stars in San Francisco. *(Still staring out at the stars:)* I don't think anyone in my family has ever gotten divorced. I turn the porch light back on—just in case Barbara needs to come home.

BARBARA'S MOM. We're lying in bed, my husband and me. I can feel my heart still beating in that other time zone. In a way, I guess I DID leave my heart in San Francisco. I think about my children—Billy at home in California, Michael in bed with him. I wonder if they wear pajamas? I tug at my old worn-out nightgown and wish for the first time in a long time that I had something nice and new to wear in bed at night. I think about Barbara—and wonder if John is in their bed tonight. *(Beat.)* I hear my husband breathing next to me, deep and long breaths… I'm amazed at his ability to sleep no matter what. The only other sound now is the ticking of his watch. It must have started working again. Hm. So time hasn't stopped, the world goes on, and pretty soon, I'll be dreaming about a time when I was a little girl, dreaming about a moment just like this one, falling asleep next to the man I've loved for as long as I can remember. For all my dreaming, all my plans…I hadn't counted on how much would really happen. I had no idea. How could I? Some days, it doesn't even feel like this is my life. *(BARBARA's MOM suddenly sits up in bed, startled:)* I don't have anyone to tell any of this to, any of it…

(Lights out on BARBARA's MOM, and then the night sky switches off also—like God turning off the last light.)

END OF SCENE TWO

SCENE THREE:
Happiness Is What You Can Bear

In the dark we hear the joyful sound of TWO CHILDREN giggling, then laughing uncontrollably. The laughter is pure, free, uncomplicated. Then slides or home movies of two children: brother and sister. Together in a bathtub (bubbles on their heads). Holding hands on Halloween (a vampire and a tiger). And finally a photo of the little boy whispering something into the girl's ear—her eyes are wide with wonder. The only sound is the continued laughter of the two children.

With that last photo of a secret being told—onstage we begin to hear TWO ADULTS laughing. The recorded sound of the children laughing fades away as the lights bump up on BILLY and BARBARA laughing uncontrollably.

We're in a loft apartment. It's beautifully spare—like a haiku poem. The furniture seems to only reveal that whoever lives here doesn't want the furniture to reveal anything about who lives here.

There's an open bottle of red wine and two glasses. The small wooden box from Scene One is open and sits nearby. BARBARA's suitcase is around too—open and messy.

It's late at night.

BARBARA *(trying not to laugh).* ...wait wait wait! Billy! That isn't even the part that's funny, that's not the punch-line—

BILLY. OK, OK. Keep going.

(They both try not to laugh.)

BARBARA *(trying to continue the joke).* OK. So! A few days after the mom left, this guy Jack sat down and wrote his mom a letter. The letter said, "Dear Mother, I'm not saying you DID take the gravy ladle from my house, and I'm not saying you DID NOT take the gravy ladle from my house. But the fact remains that a gravy ladle has been missing ever since you were here for dinner. Love, Jack."

BILLY *(laughing)*. What happened to the gravy ladle?

BARBARA *(laughing)*. Stop interrupting. I'm going to tell you. Is there more wine? *(BILLY pours more wine for both of them.)* Several days later, Jack gets a letter from his mother that went something like this: "Dear Son, I'm not saying that you DO sleep with Rob, and I'm not saying that you DO NOT sleep with Rob. But the fact remains that if Rob was sleeping in his own bed, he would have found that gravy ladle by now. Love, Mom." *(She has barely gotten the last words out and they are both laughing out of control again. They can't stop. Laughing:)* Stop it! Stop it! Wait! I can't breathe! *(Suddenly whispering loudly.)* Oh, God! Sorry! I'm being so loud, we're going to wake up Michael.

BILLY *(whispering)*. He won't wake up. Trust me. *(Yelling.)* MICHAEL CAN SLEEP THROUGH ANYTHING. *(Laughing.)* Seriously! Earthquakes, elections. He's amazing. My husband. He just sleeps. Says he doesn't remember his dreams, but I don't believe—

(BARBARA suddenly breaks down crying. It's as intense as the laughter—which kind of makes sense in the moment. BILLY goes to her, tries to hold her. Awkward.)

BILLY *(cont'd)*. Hey. Barb. Shhh. Shhh. It's OK. You're OK.

BARBARA. I can't believe she fucking died. I mean, I can't believe it, you know?

BILLY. No.

BARBARA. Well fuck her. You know? Fuck her for dying. Fuck her for not telling us!

BILLY *(pulls away)*. Barb—

BARBARA. She knew she was dying, Billy. And she didn't tell us.

BILLY. I guess she had her reasons.

BARBARA. Yeah, but she DIED—so we're never gonna KNOW the reasons. That is just so like her. I mean—JESUS!! *(Soft.)* Jesus. *(Beat.)* Thanks for letting me come. I mean, for the ticket. I wanted to see you, Billy-Boy. You know? I— *(Beat.)* I needed to get away from—everything. Everything. I just need to be with someone who I don't have to explain everything to... You're my oldest friend, Billy. Isn't that something? *(They look at each other, keep their distance. Beat. Then:)* God! I almost forgot. I have pictures of the kids for you. *(She rummages through her purse.)* School pictures. The one of Jen was taken right before she dyed her hair—thank God. But AFTER she got the nose ring. At least her hair is almost grown out again. *(She hands him two wallet-sized photos.)* I'm convinced she's some kind of cosmic test. If I can survive being Jen's mom then I can survive anything. *(BILLY is studying the two pictures.)* I think Ryan looks like you.

BILLY. Do you love them, both of them?

BARBARA *(thinking of Mom)*. You mean do I love them equally, exactly the same? No. I don't. Ryan is easier to love right now—but I don't think I love him MORE than I love Jen. Easier isn't always better. *(Beat.)* God. That sounds very Methodist! "Easier isn't always better." *(BILLY is still looking at the photos.)* He acts like you too. In case you're wondering.

BILLY. Do you think he's gay?

BARBARA. I don't know. He does like Cher. And Miss
America. *(BILLY looks up from the photos.)* He's just a
little boy. *(BILLY doesn't say anything—but he's thinking about another little boy, a little boy who was gay.)*
Ryan and Mom used to sit on her bed and talk... I tried
not to eavesdrop, but I wanted to know what they talked
about. Just a couple weeks before Mom died, she told
Ryan about every pet she'd ever had. Dogs, cats, a
bird—I never even knew she LIKED birds...fish. All of
their names. And how each one of them died. She was
so gentle with him. She was never that gentle with me.
Do you know, Mom said, "if I'd known grandkids were
going to be so great—I'd have had them first." *(BILLY
laughs.)* Later I asked Mom if Ryan reminded her of
you. She didn't like the question. Finally she told me
that she knew what I was REALLY asking and for my
information she didn't look at kids and wonder which
ones were gay. She looked at the MOTHERS—and
wondered which ones were the MOTHERS of gay
SONS. She didn't worry about the kids—she said there
were plenty of people to worry about the kids. It was the
mothers she worried about.

BILLY. What would you do?

BARBARA. If Ryan is gay? I'd worry about him. But I'll
worry about him if he's straight too. That's what moms
do. It's one of our jobs. On the plane I was reading this
article about how night-lights cause child leukemia.
Thinking about that'll keep me awake for a couple of
years. *(Beat.)* When you were little, I mean when you
were Ryan's age—did you really know that you were
gay?

BILLY. Mm, I didn't know there was a name for it. It was just—feelings. When I was seven or eight I had a crush on Jason...Jason— *(He's forgotten Jason's last name.)*

BARBARA. Jason Barrett?

BILLY. Barrett, right.

BARBARA. You had a crush on Jason Barrett? I had a crush on Jason Barrett.

BILLY. Well he was cute.

BARBARA. He WAS cute.

BILLY. I loved him.

BARBARA. Really?

BILLY. Really. I had this secret notebook: I used to copy down all of the basketball scores out of the newspaper, and write down words I wanted to remember...Verb. Treehouse. Eureka. And then there was Jason—for a while "Jason" was my favorite word. I wrote "Billy Loves Jason"—just to see how it felt, you know, how it felt to write it down. I liked it. It was scary but I liked it. And I liked that it was scary. It made me feel like I was Billy the Kid, breaking some law.

BARBARA. Well in most states you WERE breaking some law.

BILLY. I just kept writing it over and over, filling up the entire notebook with those three words: Billy Loves Jason.

BARBARA. Do you think he loved you back?

BILLY. I don't think so. But I wanted him to. I even figured out a way to be alone with him so I could kiss him.

BARBARA. Wow. You never told me that. Wasn't he older than you?

BILLY. Yeah, he was a year ahead of me in school.

BARBARA. I didn't know you went for older men.

BILLY. He was nine. Anyway: I kissed him—right on the mouth—I really kissed him—I was in heaven. I kissed him with my eyes open—and he had this funny look on his face, I thought it was the look of love. What the hell did I know? Jason said, real slow: "'Kiss'—and 'Kill'—are almost the same word." And then he beat the shit out of me.

BARBARA. Why didn't you tell me? I would have hunted him down and kicked his ass.

BILLY *(laughing)*. I guess that's why I didn't tell you. It was kind of embarrassing to always have my sister finish my fights. *(Beat.)* So after that I didn't kiss another boy for a long time.

BARBARA. Well that would do it.

BILLY. I saw him at Mom's funeral.

BARBARA. He's kind of fat, yeah?

BILLY. He didn't look at me but I talked to his wife.

BARBARA. Linda.

BILLY. LINDA sent me an e-mail after the funeral. It was one of those on-line cards—e-sympathy. The message in the e-mail said that she was sorry about Mom's death and that it was nice to see me at the funeral. She said Michael seemed like a great guy. And that although she doesn't approve of my lifestyle, she knows God loves me and so she does too.

BARBARA. Well that must be a relief. *(Beat.)* The thing about living in a small town is that it NEEDS people like you and me.

BILLY. What do you mean?

BARBARA. We're the kooks, the freaks, the weirdos... They need us so that everyone else can feel good about their awful little lives.

BILLY. You're not a weirdo.

BARBARA. No. I'm just a freak.

BILLY. I think you're being hard on yourself.

BARBARA *(sharp)*. I wasn't asking for your pity.

BILLY *(gives it right back)*. I wasn't offering any. *(Beat.)*

BARBARA *(fact)*. You know I was always the real black sheep of the family.

BILLY. Yeah right.

BARBARA. Don't rewrite the family history, Billy. I was the black sheep. You were just gay—

BILLY. Just gay???

BARBARA. —and straight as an arrow by the way. When you came out to Mom and Dad, suddenly I looked pretty damn good—which I didn't think was such a great thing. Your being gay made me seem "normal" to them—I didn't want to be normal! Suddenly I was more like them than you were. Which pissed me off because I wasn't anything like Mom and Dad...even though they treated me like I was. All of a sudden. *(Beat.)* Well this is probably a good time to give you your last present. Hope you like it. *(BARBARA tosses BILLY a plastic bag.)* Sorry I didn't wrap it.

BILLY *(pulls out a T-shirt and reads it aloud)*. "Homosexuality Is Something You're Born With—Like Red Hair or a Dead Twin." *(Laughing.)* You are so sick.

BARBARA. I bought it on the Internet. It's amazing what seems funny in the middle of the night. Maybe you can sell it on eBay.

BILLY. Sell it? No way. *(BILLY folds the T-shirt like it's something to be treasured. They both sip their wine. They're quiet. Then:)* I always thought Dad would die first.

BARBARA. Yeah.

BILLY. I don't know if he can get along without Mom.

BARBARA. I don't know if I can take care of him either.

BILLY. What do you mean? No one's asking you to take care of him.

BARBARA. Billy—

BILLY. He's in good health, he's not even that old.

BARBARA. Neither was Mom. *(Beat.)* He stopped wearing his watch.

BILLY. So? Maybe it broke. He's had it forever.

BARBARA. No. He says he lost it.

BILLY. People lose things.

BARBARA. At the funeral, I saw him slip off his watch and tuck it into the casket.

BILLY. Maybe you didn't see it right.

BARBARA. What do you mean?

BILLY. Maybe it wasn't his watch, maybe it wasn't anything.

BARBARA. Why are you being so stupid? I told you what I saw: He buried his watch with Mom. Why would I make that up?

BILLY *(quick)*. Why would he say he lost it?

BARBARA *(quick)*. Why didn't Mom tell us she was dying? *(Beat.)* How did I not know? How did she keep that a secret from me, from us?

BILLY *(tired, trying to be patient)*. I don't know, Barb. It's not like we didn't keep secrets from her.

BARBARA *(not backing down)*. Stop confusing me with the facts! I've made up my mind. And that's not the point anyway. I can't believe you're not pissed that she didn't tell us—

BILLY. I didn't say I'm not pissed—

BARBARA. Well are you?

BILLY. Obviously you want me to be.

BARBARA. No!

BILLY. You mean—

BARBARA. I mean, not if you're NOT pissed. But I don't see how you CAN'T be pissed.

BILLY. You mean I should be pissed because you're pissed—

BARBARA. She lied to us—

BILLY. She didn't LIE!—she—just didn't tell us the truth.

BARBARA. Oh Christ.

BILLY. What?!? Sometimes lying and not telling the truth are two different things.

BARBARA. Well that's something you would know all about.

BILLY. What's that supposed to mean?

BARBARA. Why did you tell me first? Why did you tell me you were gay—

BILLY. Because I trusted you!

BARBARA. Well it was a burden—keeping your secret from everyone.

BILLY. I was a kid, I was scared, I didn't know what was going to happen. I wanted to know somebody loved me.

BARBARA. Loved you? Loved YOU? The Golden Son? God, Billy. Of course we loved you. Even after you left! Then they just loved you more.

BILLY. I didn't leave—I just didn't stay.

BARBARA. No— No, you left!

BILLY. Barb—

BARBARA. You left! You left ME! You left me to deal with Mom and Dad all by myself.

BILLY. I was trying to live my life.

BARBARA. Lucky you. While you were off living your
    life I had to do all the dirty work.

BILLY. What dirty work?

BARBARA. Somebody had to raise Mom and Dad. Do
    you think they just grew up because they WANTED
    to??? You don't get it. Do you think they would have—
    (She stops herself.)

BILLY. Would have what?

(They stare at each other. Then:)

BARBARA. It was a lot of work, Billy. And whenever you
    DID come home, we were all expected to drop whatever
    we were doing because "Billy's Home!" and what could
    be more important than that?

BILLY. I never expected you to drop everything—

BARBARA. But THEY did. Mom and Dad expected it.
    You'd show up and it was always a feast, always an
    event, a celebration…and everyone was expected to
    bend our lives around you…time stopped whenever you
    came home. And it wouldn't start again until you were
    gone. Mom and Dad made up everything they didn't
    know about you and your life. They filled in the gaps
    with gold instead of cement.

*(BILLY doesn't know what to say. He's as frustrated as
BARBARA is pissed off.)*

BILLY. Sorry? *(Beat.)* What do you want me to say?

BARBARA. Say that she's not really dead! Say that Dad's
    going to be OK! Say that you're not going to disappear
    out of my life! Say that my kids don't hate me now and

that they won't hate me when they grow up! Say that
I'm pretty! Say that somebody's going to want to kiss
me. Say that I'm going to want to kiss them back! Say
that being single with two kids doesn't mean I won't
ever have sex again! And if I ever DO have sex again
say that I'll enjoy it! Fuck! I don't know. Say that I remind you of Julia Roberts and not Julia Child... *(BILLY
is laughing and crying.)* Say it. *(BILLY doesn't know if
she's serious.)* SAY IT!!!

BILLY. You remind me of Julia Roberts and not Julia
Child.

BARBARA. Really?

BILLY. Cross my heart. *(Beat.)*

BARBARA. I wanted to send out announcements for the
divorce but John refused to pay for half. I was just as
happy to divorce him as I was to marry him.

BILLY. What really happened between you and asshole I
mean John?

BARBARA. Not much. And that was the problem. I was
literally bored to tears, Billy. I was crying all the time—
crying, crying crying and I finally figured out it was because I was bored. The final straw was a day when I
was on the phone with the gas company. Our check had
bounced. I was on hold...and there was recorded music
playing, it was an old John Denver song, some love
song that he'd written for his wife. And I started crying
because I remembered that John Denver had gotten divorced. And then I remembered that John Denver had
died. And I wondered if it was the divorce that had
killed him—or the marriage. Maybe I did marry John to
prove I wasn't such a screw-up. So getting divorced,
even though it's the best thing—for everyone—some

days it just feels like such a failure, like I'M such a failure.

BILLY. You're not a failure—

BARBARA. I want to change things, Billy. I want to live my life. Like you. Only different.

BILLY. Do you and John talk?

BARBARA. About the kids. But he's already out having his fun, being single. I'm kind of relieved to tell you the truth. I like John more now that I don't have to love him anymore. That seems like a step in the right direction. But I don't think you ever really get over your first liar. *(They don't say anything for a moment.)* What about you and Michael? How are the happy newlyweds?

BILLY. Well—we're not married anymore either.

BARBARA. What?!

BILLY. Legally. We're not legally married. The courts threw all the marriage licenses out the window. They took away our membership, asked for the keys, and locked us out of the mainstream again.

BARBARA. That sucks. You want to be in the club and they won't let you. I don't want to be in the club and they won't let me out.

BILLY. I liked having that piece of paper, Barb. I don't know why. I liked being married. I miss it in a weird way.

BARBARA. But you're together, right? You're married. I mean fuck the government. What a bunch of hypocrites.

BILLY *(genuine)*. You are the best sister in the world. My hero.

BARBARA. Too much pressure. Just say I'm pretty.

BILLY. You're pretty.

BARBARA. Thank you. *(Beat.)*

BILLY. I cheated on Michael.

BARBARA. What?

BILLY. I fucked up.

BARBARA. Does he know?

BILLY. Yeah. He knows. Everybody knows.

BARBARA. Are you guys gonna be OK?

BILLY. I think so. I hope so. I really do love him. That's the thing that's so crazy, Barb. I go out of my way to be nice to strangers—and I hurt the person I love the most.

BARBARA. So you're not perfect. What a relief.

BILLY. I don't feel much relief.

BARBARA. Not you—me. It's a relief to ME that you're not perfect.

BILLY *(the truth)*. I'm not. *(Beat.)* Did you ever cheat on John?

BARBARA. No—but I wanted to. I should have.

BILLY. Probably not. I don't recommend it.

(Beat. BARBARA looks around the spare room.)

BARBARA. I like your apartment.

BILLY. Thanks.

BARBARA. It's like something in a magazine. I mean I don't know how you LIVE here, but I like it. It's a little too—

BILLY. Perfect?

BARBARA. I didn't want to say it. *(Self-conscious.)* Sorry about my mess. I just kind of dumped everything.

BILLY. It's OK. I like having you here.

BARBARA. Oh God! I forgot to call Dad. I want to make sure he's OK. Ryan is staying at the house with him while I'm away. He'll have homework.

BILLY. Sure. *(BILLY goes to the phone.)*

BARBARA. The other day I was signing a permission slip for Ryan to go on a field trip and he said, "Every kid in my class knows his mom's number at work. None of us knows our dad's number. It was really funny, Mom." I said, "Yeah. Really funny, son."

BILLY *(on phone)*. Dad? Hi. It's Billy. Bill. No, every-thing's fine. God, sorry—I forgot about the time differ-ence. *(To BARBARA.)* I woke him up.

BARBARA *(whispering)*. Shit!

BILLY *(to phone)*. Yeah, she got here in one piece, she's fine. Actually she's great. *(Beat.)* Everything OK there? *(Awkward beat.)* How's the weather? Is it hot? Uh-huh. Right. *(Awkward beat.)* Michael says hi. *(Beat.)* I'll tell him. *(Awkward beat.)* OK. *(Awkward beat.)* Well. *(Awk-ward beat.)* I'll put Barbara on, she wants to talk to you. *(BILLY quickly hands BARBARA the phone.)*

BARBARA *(on phone, talking non-stop)*. Dad? Hey! How are you? Are you eating? Did you eat dinner? You found all the food I put in the freezer, right? Uh- huh... yeah... Yeah but I made all those little dinners and froze them in individual containers. No, just microwave them for five-and-a-half minutes. I didn't put any salt in it. *(Beat.)* That's fine but just remember what the doctor said. *(BILLY is standing to the side watching BARBARA in amazement. On phone:)* Did Ryan get to school on time this morning? No he's not very cheerful in the morning. How late did he stay up? That's too late...well he's lying, he does not get to stay up that late on a school night. I'm sure he did. No, don't wake him. I'll call him tomorrow. Yeah, I gave them to Billy. I know. I told him the same thing. *(Beat.)* Wow. *(To BILLY.)* Dad

says that Ryan has your handwriting too. *(To phone.)*
How much homework did he have? Oh God, Dad—I'm
sorry. Did you understand any of it? I usually have to
fake my way through the math. *(Listening.)* Very im-
pressive. Has Jen been by? *(Sharp.)* What?!? How big is
it? Oh, Christ. Where is it? *(Explaining to BILLY.)* Jen
got a tattoo. *(On phone.)* Did you tell her it was the stu-
pidest thing she's ever done? Why not? Well I can't
think of a stupider thing, can you? OK. Whatever. I'll
deal with her when I get home. *(Laughing.)* Thanks,
Dad. You sure you're OK? Good. You want to say
goodbye to Billy? Love you too. *(BARBARA hands the
phone to BILLY.)*

BILLY *(on phone)*. Hey, Dad. OK. I will. *(Beat.)* Dad?
(Beat.) Love you. *(Beat.)* Bye.

*(BILLY hangs up the phone. BARBARA stretches, looks
out a window at the lights of the city. BILLY pours the
last drops of wine into his glass.)*

BARBARA *(still looking out the window)*. I wasn't much
older than Jen when I had my abortion and I get completely bent out shape because she gets a tattoo. *(Beat.)*
How did Mom do it? How did she—survive me?
(Thinking about it.) Oh right. She didn't. *(Beat.)* I talk to
her, to Mom. Hell, I even fight with her. When I was
waiting for you at the airport, I just sat on my suitcase—
and started fighting with Mom, just like always. I feel
like I can forgive her for dying as long as we're still
fighting about it. When she stops fighting with me…
How long did she know she was dying? How long did
Dad know? What else does he know that he's not telling

us? I was there, Billy. I see her—I saw her every day.
How did I miss it?

BILLY. You missed it because she didn't want you to see
it.

BARBARA. Fine! So she didn't want me to see it. *(Beat.)*
Why? *(BILLY doesn't have the answer. No one does.
BILLY goes to the small wooden box and brings it to
sofa. BARBARA continues.)* I can't believe you lugged
that all the way back here.

BILLY. It's the only thing I really wanted. Dad told me
that when we were born, he got each of us a fifty-dollar
U.S. Savings Bond.

BARBARA. Believe me—I cashed mine in a long time
ago.

BILLY. Dad got us savings bonds—and Mom got both of
us a box.

BARBARA. It's a hope chest. *(BILLY looks at her, know-
ingly.)* You give them to people when they get married.
Hope chest. Mom gave me mine when I got married.
Not that it did any good.

BILLY. Well she never gave me mine. And I wanted it.
What was in yours?

BARBARA. Oh you know, Mom stuff. *The Joy of
Cooking.* A book of baby names just in case I didn't
know how much she wanted grandkids. A necklace that
belonged to Grandma. I don't remember everything.
What's in yours?

BILLY. Not much. *(He pulls out the child's self-portrait
from Scene One.)* This picture I drew of myself when I
was little.

BARBARA *(looks at the drawing).* Why'd you give yourself yellow hair?

BILLY *(puzzled)*. I don't know. I can't remember. *(He pulls out a few more things:)* The wedding invitation I sent Mom and Dad. The picture of me and Michael kissing at our wedding. And this little piece of scrap paper with Mom's handwriting. *(He hands the little piece of paper to BARBARA. She looks at it.)*

BARBARA. It's a receipt.

BILLY. Turn it over.

BARBARA *(turns the piece of paper over. Reading it aloud)*. "Happiness is what you can bear." *(Beat.)* Happiness is what you can bear. *(Beat.)* What the fuck does that mean?

BILLY. I don't know. I've been trying to figure it out. It could mean a lot of things. It could mean everything. *(Beat.)* Happiness is what you can bear. *(Beat.)* Do you think Mom was happy?

BARBARA. I guess…in her way. But I think she was lonely too. If she didn't tell US everything, how do we know she told Dad everything? And if she didn't tell him, who did she tell? I don't even know if she believed in God. *(BARBARA stretches out on the sofa, puts her head in BILLY's lap.)* Remember how we used to leave phone messages for each other—pretending we were Mom and Dad. That was fun. You had Mom down. *(Beat.)* Billy? Tell me a story about Mom.

(BILLY thinks about it. He pulls the stamped, hand-addressed wedding invitation out of the box:)

BILLY. Well…it's a wedding invitation. Anyone can see that. It came in the mail mixed up with a VISA bill, and a newsletter from my church, a couple of offers for unlimited night minutes if you switch to a different long-distance carrier, and a two-dollar coupon off a certain brand of cheese. *(Still with her head in her brother's lap, BARBARA laughs softly.)* I saw the wedding invitation right away because it was the only envelope with a handwritten address. Have you noticed how we just don't get that much handwritten mail anymore? Everyone's just so busy. *(He looks at the wedding invitation.)* The stamp is one of those "LOVE" stamps. My son used to collect stamps. He'd say that getting a stamp from some far-away country made him feel like he'd get to go there someday… *(BILLY stops. He's crying.)*

BARBARA. Billy? You OK?

BILLY. Not really. *(Beat.)* But I will be. *(Beat.)*

BARBARA. When?

BILLY. I don't know.

BARBARA. In the morning?

BILLY. Maybe. *(Beat.)* I hope so. *(The lights begin to fade slowly. BARBARA snuggles deeper into BILLY's lap. BILLY is touching her hair. He's trying to stop crying. It's going to take a while. Trying to push through his tears.)* It was the handwriting that I recognized. It's my son's handwriting. He probably doesn't want me to tell you this but for years I kept a picture that Billy drew for me when he was a little boy…

(It's dark now. It won't be morning for a long time. BILLY's still crying. BARBARA holds on tight.)

END OF PLAY